13 most important BIBLE Lessons

for kids about God

Group

Loveland, Colorado
group.com

Group resources really work!

This Group resource incorporates our R.E.A.L. approach to ministry. It reinforces a growing friendship with Jesus, encourages long-term learning, and results in life transformation, because it's

Relational
Learner-to-learner interaction enhances learning and builds Christian friendships.

Experiential
What learners experience through discussion and action sticks with them up to 9 times longer than what they simply hear or read.

Applicable
The aim of Christian education is to equip learners to be both hearers and doers of God's Word.

Learner-based
Learners understand and retain more when the learning process takes into consideration how they learn best.

Visit our website: group.com

CREDITS
Contributing Authors:
Jody Brolsma, Dave Thornton,
Courtney Walsh, and Vicki L.O. Witte
Editors:
Lee Sparks, Ann Diaz, and Andrea Zimmerman
Cover Design:
Rebecca Parrott
Book Design:
Jean Bruns

Unless otherwise indicated, all Scripture quotations are taken from the *Holy Bible,* New Living Translation, copyright © 1996, 2004, 2007. Used by permission of Tyndale House Publishers, Inc. Carol Stream, Illinois 60188. All rights reserved.

ISBN 978-0-7644-7066-0

13 12 11 10 9 8   23 22 21 20 19

Printed in the United States of America.

CONTENTS

3

INTRODUCTION

Ask people who minister to children what they want most and you'll hear something like this: "I want kids to know the Bible." "I want children to have a strong relationship with God." "I want kids to have a faith foundation that'll stand the test of time."

That's what *13 Most Important Bible Lessons for Kids About God* is all about—helping kids build a strong foundation in the basics of their faith. You'll find 13 lessons that'll bring kids face to face with God as you help them discover answers to these important faith foundation questions: Who is God? Who is Jesus? Who is the Holy Spirit? We've chosen 13 attributes of God, Jesus, and the Holy Spirit that drill down to the very bedrock of the Christian faith.

These faith foundations won't fill your kids with theoretical information they won't retain. Instead, the lessons are designed to transform your kids by engaging them in learning activities that'll help them know the loving God who created them and sustains them.

There are three sections in this book:

Who Is God? The first section covers the idea of the Trinity, God's goodness, God's holiness, and how God is everlasting. This section covers key attributes for understanding who God is.

Who Is Jesus? The second section looks at Jesus' incarnation (God in human flesh), Jesus' humble power, his existence since the beginning of Creation, Jesus' paying for our sins with his death, and Jesus' victory of death in the resurrection. These five attributes of Jesus are basic to the Christian faith.

Who Is the Holy Spirit? The final section covers how the Holy Spirit guides and teaches, advocates for us, is present always, and equips and gifts Christians. Kids will learn key attributes about the Holy Spirit.

Here's the flow for each lesson:

Set the Foundation—Engage kids in an opening activity to get them enthused and wanting more.

7

Present the Bible Foundation—This is the "meat" of the lesson, designed to help kids dig into the Bible.

Build on the Foundation—Once kids have learned a key attribute of God, they respond and apply what they've learned in a meaningful way.

Jesus told a much-loved children's ministry Bible story about the need to build a strong faith foundation. You know the story: The wise man built his house upon the rock...and nothing could tear down that house!

This is what you dream of, plan for, and pray about in ministry—that the children you minister to will have such a strong faith foundation that nothing will be able to tear down their faith. May God use *13 Most Important Bible Lessons for Kids About God* and you to lead children in their growing relationship with God, Jesus, and the Holy Spirit.

Be aware that some children have food allergies that can be dangerous. Know your children, and consult with parents about allergies their children may have. Also be sure to read food labels carefully as hidden ingredients can cause allergy-related problems.

To avoid choking hazards, be sure to pick up pieces of any broken balloons promptly. Balloons may contain latex.

God Is Three in One

T he Trinity has been described by some theologians as the Divine Riddle: "One makes three and three makes one." This essential aspect of the nature of God as three in one is important for children to know and understand. The word *trinity* is a shortened version of *tri-unity*. Although the Trinity isn't found in the Bible, the truth of God as three in one is scattered throughout the pages of Scripture. In this lesson, you'll help kids discover that God really is three in one and that they can have a friendship with the one God who is God the Father, Son, and Holy Spirit.

Scripture Foundation

2 CORINTHIANS 13:14
God the Father, God the Son, and God the Holy Spirit work together.

DEUTERONOMY 6:4
Moses reminds the people that the Lord is our God and the Lord is one.

MATTHEW 28:19
Just before ascending into heaven, Jesus instructs his disciples to baptize all nations in the name of the Father, Son, and Holy Spirit.

JOHN 14:9
Jesus tells us that anyone who has seen him has seen God.

JOHN 14:16-17
Jesus promises that God will send the Helper, "the Spirit of truth."

THIS LESSON AT A GLANCE

SEQUENCE	EXPERIENCES	SUPPLIES
SET THE FOUNDATION (about 10 minutes)	***Perfect Agreement*** Kids will form trios and move through an obstacle course to experience working as three in one.	• various items for making a simple obstacle course
PRESENT THE BIBLE FOUNDATION (about 25 minutes)	***Different but the Same*** Kids will peel hard-boiled eggs to connect the idea of God as three in one.	• Bibles • 1 hard-boiled egg per child • 1 plate per child • napkins • wet wipes • crayons or stickers
BUILD ON THE FOUNDATION (about 10 minutes)	***Trinity Shield*** Kids will each personalize a Trinity shield drawing and then share their responses with a friend.	• a copy of "Trinity Shield" hand-out for each child (p. 15) • crayons or markers • *optional:* CD of soft worship music, CD player

Before the Lesson

SET THE FOUNDATION: *Perfect Agreement*—Establish a simple obstacle course in your meeting area or a park if possible. Use chairs, tables, and other common items. If at a park, have kids go around a tree, under a swing, over the merry-go-round twice, and so on to return to the starting place. Choose safe and easy obstacles.

Perfect Agreement

(about 10 minutes)

SAY:

A long time ago, Christians would repeat a statement each week when they gathered for worship. They said something like this: "So the Father is God, the Son is God, and the Holy Spirit is God. And yet there aren't three Gods but one God." Let's play a game to learn more about God as three in one.

Form trios. Have kids each choose one of these roles in their trios: Eyes (this person is the only one who can have open eyes), Feet (this person leads the way by taking steps while the other two follow), Mouth (this person hears directions from the Eyes and whispers to the Feet). Have trios move through the obstacle course. Allow a few minutes for the game.

ASK:

• What was it like moving through the obstacle course with your trio?

• What did your trio have to do to get back to the starting point?

SAY:

Just as there were three of you teamed up in this game, there are three persons in God—God the Father, God the Son, and God the Holy Spirit.

Read aloud 2 Corinthians 13:14. John 14:16-17 and John 16:13.

SAY:

In these passages, we get a glimpse of what God the Father, God the Son, and God the Holy Spirit do.

ASK:

• What do you learn about the Father, Son, and Holy Spirit's roles in these Scriptures?

• Which roles in your trio match the roles of the different parts of the Trinity?

11

LESSON 1: God Is Three in One

- **Just as in our game, why is it important that each part of the Trinity does the right part?**

SAY:

It's hard to understand how God can be three persons and still be one God. But that's what the Bible tells us about God. Let's look more closely at what it means for God to be three in one.

Different but the Same

(about 25 minutes)

SAY:

Before we look at what the Bible says about God as three in one, let's take a look at how something can be different but the same.

Pass out a hard-boiled egg and a plate to each child. Have crayons or stickers available to decorate eggs.

SAY:

Let's decorate these eggs with symbols or pictures of what you think represents God, Jesus, and the Holy Spirit from these Scriptures.

Have kids read Deuteronomy 6:4, Matthew 28:19, John 14:9, and John 14:16-17. Have kids decorate their eggs based on what they've read in these Scriptures. When it appears that most kids have finished decorating their eggs, ask willing kids to share their decorations with the entire group.

SAY:

Great job decorating your eggs. Now I want to show you something.

12

Take your own egg, with the shell still on, and cut it into halves with a serrated knife. Hold up the halves so kids can see them.

ALLERGY
ALERT

See page 8

ASK:

• How are the three parts different or the same?

• Why is each part dependent on the other three?

SAY:

Like the egg, God is three parts: Father, Son, and Holy Spirit. The shell can represent Jesus, whose body was fragile and broken. The yolk can represent God, who is set apart as holy from humans and is also the center. Finally, the egg white connects the shell with the yolk, which can represent the Holy Spirit.

Invite kids to have the egg as a snack, gently cracking the shell and enjoying the contents of the egg. Pass out napkins and wet wipes.

SAY:

Now that we've seen how the Trinity, like the egg, has three parts that form one whole, let's build on that.

BUILD ON THE FOUNDATION

Trinity Shield

(about 10 minutes)

Pass out a copy of the "Trinity Shield" handout to each child, along with markers or crayons. Play soft worship music in the background while kids draw, if you wish.

SAY:

Let's respond to God as three in one by coloring this Trinity shield.

SAY:

Take a few minutes to draw a picture or write words that describe what you think about God's unique role in your life as Father, Son, or Holy Spirit. For God as Father you might draw a picture or write something

13

about how he created the world or your body. For the Son or Jesus you might draw a picture of Jesus on the cross or rising from the empty tomb. For the Holy Spirit you might draw a dove or write something about how God comforts you when you're sad.

After giving kids 10 minutes to personalize their shields, ask them to pair up with a friend. Ask each of them to spend a few minutes sharing their pictures or words and talking about how they feel about God in each of the unique parts of the Trinity. After each child has had a turn to talk, ask kids to sit and hold their pictures while they pray silently and thank God for creating, saving, and comforting them.

For your closing prayer, have kids each think of one word of thanks about each of the three-in-one aspects of God.

PRAY:

God the Father, thanks for creating me. When I think about how you created me and the beautiful world we live in, the one word I want to tell you is…[let kids say a word].

God the Son, Jesus, thanks for coming to earth. When I think about how you lived your life, died on the cross, and then rose from the grave, the one word I want to say to you is…[let kids say a word].

God the Holy Spirit, thanks for living inside me. When I think about how you help me be more like you, I want to tell you…[let kids say a word].

Close your time together with the benediction from 2 Corinthians 13:14. Point out to kids that if they listen, they'll hear in this one verse each specific name of our three-in-one God: **"May the grace of the Lord Jesus Christ, the love of God, and the fellowship of the Holy Spirit be with you all."**

14

Trinity Shield

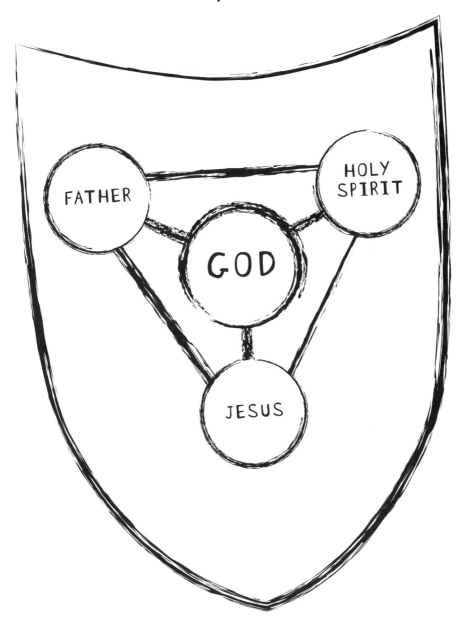

LESSON 1: God Is Three in One

God Is Good

For many kids, one of the first meal-time prayers they learn celebrates God's greatness as well as his goodness: "God is great. God is good. Now we thank God for this food." This wonderful truth about God summarizes so many other aspects of his character, including his moral purity, his integrity, and his love. In this lesson, kids will begin to understand that God is good—and will be invited to respond to God's goodness and love by thanking him.

Scripture Foundation

GENESIS 1:31-2:4
God's creation is good.

NEHEMIAH 9:13-15
God's commands are good.

PSALM 34:8
We can experience God's goodness with all our senses.

EZEKIEL 34:11-15
God is the good shepherd.

ROMANS 5:6-8
God gives up his life even for enemies.

3 JOHN 11
We can imitate God because he is good.

THIS LESSON AT A GLANCE

SEQUENCE	EXPERIENCES	SUPPLIES
SET THE FOUNDATION (about 10 minutes)	**Good Shepherd Tag** Kids will play a version of the Red Rover game as they experience that the Good Shepherd loves and cares for them.	• Bibles
PRESENT THE BIBLE FOUNDATION (about 25 minutes)	**God Is Good** Kids will take a quick quiz and then explore what the Bible says about God's goodness.	• Bibles
BUILD ON THE FOUNDATION (about 10 minutes)	**Tasty Good** Kids will enjoy a tasty apple snack as they reflect on God's goodness.	• sliced or dried apples • notecards • pencils or crayons

Before the Lesson

BUILD ON THE FOUNDATION: *Tasty Good*— Prepare enough apple slices to serve each child several.

Good Shepherd Tag

(about 10 minutes)

Gather kids together in a large open area to explain the game.

SAY:

God is like a good shepherd who works hard to keep all of his sheep safe and close to him. We're going to play a game to see how the shepherd herds his sheep.

Choose one child or adult helper to be the Shepherd. Then form two groups of approximately equal size. Have the groups line up on opposite sides of the playing area. Place the Shepherd in the middle of the playing area. The Shepherd will call for the Sheep by yelling "Come, Sheep!" The Sheep will try to run to the other side of the playing area without being caught by the Shepherd. Both sides will run simultaneously so that the two groups change sides. The Shepherd will try to tag the Sheep as they run by.

Any children who are tagged by the Shepherd will become part of the herd and help the Shepherd catch Sheep. Remind the children to be careful not to run into each other. Continue to play until all the Sheep have been tagged and the herd has been restored.

Then have kids form pairs; give each pair a Bible, and have partners read aloud Ezekiel 34:11-15.

ASK:
- **How was the way we played our game like the way God is described here as the good shepherd?**
- **What's the difference between a good shepherd and a bad one?**

SAY:

How great it is to know that God is good and loves us just like a shepherd cares for his sheep!

God Is Good

(about 25 minutes)

SAY:
Let's see how fast you can play the Good or Bad game. I'll call out an item and you need to shout out quickly if it's good or bad. Ready?
Family
Sun
Death
Friends
Dog
Enemies
Food
Bed
Bullies
Doctor
Sickness

ASK:
• How did you know so quickly if things were good or bad?

SAY:
Today we're going to both see and taste that God is good. Form trios, and I'll give each trio one of the "good" words we just looked at. Your assignment is to come up with at least three ways you know your item's good. Have groups each report back after they've had three minutes to come up with their list.

SAY:
Now I'm going to give each trio a few Bible verses to look up. Your job is to figure out how your verses show that God is good and then come up with a quick mini-drama or pantomime to show the other kids how you know God is good based on that verse. Give each group one of the

following Scriptures. It's okay to assign the same passage to more than one group.

Genesis 1:31–2:4

Nehemiah 9:13-15

Ezekiel 34:11-15

Give kids at least five minutes to come up with their ideas of how the passage shows God is good and to plan their mini-drama. Then have them share their dramas and discuss how their verses showed God's goodness.

ASK:

• **What did you learn about how good God is?**

SAY:

Here's something amazing about God's goodness. Listen to Romans 5:6-8. Read the passage aloud. **God's love and goodness are so great that he sent his Son Jesus to die for us even while we were still sinners. Can you imagine making a big sacrifice for the meanest bully you've ever known? Next to impossible, right? But this is what our good God chose to do. He offered his Son Jesus as a sacrifice for our sins even while we were still sinning. Let's see if we can taste just how good God is!**

BUILD ON THE FOUNDATION

Tasty Good

(about 10 minutes)

Bring out the apple slices. Read aloud Psalm 34:8.

SAY:

As I pass out the apple slices, call out all the good things God does for you. Pass out the apple slices, allowing kids to call out things like "gives me my family," "takes care of my dog," "died on the cross," or "gives us food."

See page 8

21

SAY:

God is so good and he demonstrates his love and goodness to us in so many ways but especially by giving us the gift of his Son Jesus, who died on the cross for us. One of the best ways we can respond to the taste of God's goodness is to thank him. For every apple slice you eat, think of five good things you can thank God for this week. If kids want to, they can write their ideas on notecards.

After a few moments, lead kids in prayer.

PRAY:

Dear God, thank you for being so very good to us. Your goodness and love are amazing. In Jesus' name, amen.

LESSON 3

God Is Holy

T he concept of God's holiness can be hard for kids to grasp. It's hard for most adults to fully understand. Perhaps we struggle to communicate that God is holy to kids. In an effort to help kids discover God's incredible love and grace, it's possible that we downplay God's holiness. God's holiness—his purity, righteousness, and divinity—don't make him cold and distant. Yet the fact that God is holy *does* impact our relationship with him. How do we interact with a sacred and sinless God? How can we respond to a perfect and faithful God? As you lead kids through these discoveries, you'll open their eyes to how amazing our holy and perfect God really is.

Scriptural Foundation

EXODUS 3:2-5
God tells Moses to take off his sandals.

EXODUS 19:9-11
Moses prepares the people to hear God.

THIS LESSON AT A GLANCE

SEQUENCE	EXPERIENCES	SUPPLIES
SET THE FOUNDATION (about 10 minutes)	*Fine Dining* Kids will compare casual and fancy dining place settings to explore how we celebrate something incredible.	• paper or foam cup • paper plate • plastic fork • fancy, china dish (or entire place setting) • fancy glass • silver (or stainless steel) fork • 2 trays
PRESENT THE BIBLE FOUNDATION (about 25 minutes)	*Holy Ground* Kids will take off their shoes and then choose words that could also mean *holy*.	• Bibles • wet wipes • markers • white paper
BUILD ON THE FOUNDATION (about 10 minutes)	*Fingerprints* Kids will create fingerprint pictures of themselves leading holy lives.	• washable ink pads (1 for every 3 kids) • paper • wet wipes • *optional:* CD of reflective music, CD player

Before the Lesson

SET THE FOUNDATION: *Fine Dining* — On a tray, set out a place setting of a paper plate, paper or foam cup, and plastic fork. On another tray, set out a place setting of fancy china, a silver fork, and a glass water goblet. Set the trays out of sight but where you can easily retrieve them.

Fine Dining

(about 10 minutes)

Form a circle.

SAY:

Think of a time you had a fancy or special meal. It may've been on a holiday or during a time your parents took you to a special restaurant. Think for a minute about what that was like. Pause for a few seconds so kids can think.

I want to hear about your experience, but we'll do it rapid-fire! That means I'll start a sentence and we'll go around the circle and let each person answer quickly, with one or two words that finish the sentence.

One at a time, start the following sentences and let kids go around the circle so each person can complete the sentence. Encourage kids to have fun answering quickly.

SAY:

For this meal, we went to...

The food was served on plates that were...

The table was covered with...

The forks, knives, and spoons were...

We drank from cups that were...

My parents expected me to act...

ASK:

• **How did all of those elaborate dishes and tablecloths and things make the experience feel different?**

SAY:

I'm guessing that none of you ate on something that looked like this.

Set the paper place setting in the middle of the circle.

ASK:

• **When would you use something like this?**

25

Bring out the china place setting and set it in the middle of the circle.

ASK:
• Why do people use fancy or special dishes like these?

SAY:
The paper plates are fine—they have a purpose for things like camping or backyard barbecues. But when you want to show people they're special or celebrate something incredible, you'd use the fancy plates. Today we're going to explore that God is holy. *Holy* means set apart or special…sort of like these china dishes. We'll see that the Bible talks a lot about how holy, perfect, pure, and righteous God is.

Move both place settings out of sight.

PRESENT THE BIBLE FOUNDATION

Holy Ground

(about 25 minutes)

SAY:
One of the first times the Bible tells us about God's holiness is when Moses heard from God. Moses was a shepherd then, out taking care of his father-in-law's sheep; he saw a bush on fire…but not burning up! God used that burning bush to get Moses' attention. Listen to what happened.

Read aloud Exodus 3:4-5 from a kid-friendly translation of the Bible.

ASK:
• What do you think God meant by "holy ground"? What was so special about that soil?

26

SAY:

God is so perfect and holy that even the ground he touches is special!

Ask kids to take off their shoes and sit in a circle.

SAY:

Taking off shoes was just a start. Later, when Moses led God's people—the Israelites—God wanted to prove to the Israelites that Moses wasn't just making all these things up. God wanted the Israelites to hear his voice. God's presence is so holy and perfect that the people needed to keep a little bit of distance from it.

Lead kids in reading Exodus 19:9-11.

ASK:

• **Tell about a time you had to clean up before doing something.**

• **Why do you think the people had to do all those things?**

SAY:

We're going to learn a little more about what it means that God is holy. But maybe you'd better clean up first.

Hand out wet wipes for kids to wash their hands. (Or if your room is near a restroom, let kids go and use actual soap and water for a more memorable experience.)

Form three groups and give each group a Bible, a pen, and a white sheet of paper. Assign one of the following Scriptures to each group, and then have groups move apart as they read their assigned passages. Ask kids to read the passage and then write two words or phrases they could use in place of the word *holy* in that Bible verse.

Psalm 99:3-5

Luke 11:1-2

Revelation 4:8

Allow about five minutes for kids to read and work on their passages. Then bring kids back to the circle, and have groups read aloud their assigned passages, set their papers on the floor, and explain why they chose the words they did.

ASK:

• **Why is God holy? What would the world be like if God *wasn't* holy?**

• **What do you think about God being** [read some of the words kids wrote down]**?**

27

SAY:

God is holy, [say some of the words kids wrote down]. **But he's also merciful and loving to us, his creations. It's incredible to think that God reaches out to us, cares what we think and feel, and wants to spend forever with us. Let's explore how knowing that can change our hearts.**

BUILD ON THE FOUNDATION

Fingerprints

(about 10 minutes)

ASK:
• **Tell whether you'd consider yourself holy or not.**

SAY:
Most of us don't think of ourselves as holy. We make mistakes. We disobey. We don't feel very [use some of the words kids added in the previous activity]. **But God created us with his holy hands. If God can make soil holy—set apart for a special purpose—God can make us holy. In fact, God *wants* us to be holy.**

Read aloud 2 Timothy 1:9.

ASK:
• **What does a holy life look like?**

SAY:
Think about God's holy hands creating you. He gave you your eyes, mind, hands, and feet. Turn to a partner and tell how you can use those things to live a holy life.

Allow time for sharing.

28

SAY:

Now use this stamp pad and your fingerprints to create a picture of yourself leading a holy life, or something that reminds you to be holy, or even just your name.

Give each child a sheet of paper. If possible, have a washable ink stamp pad for every three kids, so kids can spread out and spend a few minutes reflecting as they make their fingerprint pictures. Play quiet, reflective music while kids work (optional). After at least five minutes, hand out wet wipes and let kids wipe the ink off their fingers.

PRAY:

Holy God, you are so perfect, pure, and special—it's hard for us to believe that you love us. Lord, show us how we can live holy lives, the way you've planned for us. Help us live as people who bear your fingerprints on all that we do and all that we are. In Jesus' name, amen.

God Is Everlasting

I n a child's world, there aren't a lot of things that last. Technology changes constantly, families move, parents' jobs change, and fads come and go. And it's not just their surroundings that evolve. To children—whose bodies and minds are ever-growing, ever-changing—it makes sense that things have a limited "life." They're used to outgrowing everything from clothing to schoolbooks to bicycles! No wonder it's challenging for kids to wrap their brains around the idea that God has always been, exists now, and will always be. In this lesson, kids will get the eye-opening reassurance that God has been around forever…and will continue into eternity.

Scripture Foundation

PSALM 39:4
Our lives are just a moment—a breath—compared to God's.

REVELATION 1:8
God is the beginning and the end.

1 CHRONICLES 16:36
God lives from everlasting to everlasting.

1 TIMOTHY 1:17
God never dies.

THIS LESSON AT A GLANCE

SEQUENCE	EXPERIENCES	SUPPLIES
SET THE FOUNDATION (about 10 minutes)	***Ring Around*** Kids will pass a hoop around the circle and talk about how a circle has no start or end.	• hula hoop • jump-rope or 6-foot length of rope
PRESENT THE BIBLE FOUNDATION (about 25 minutes)	***On and On and On*** Kids will use Scripture and crepe paper to compare our short lives to God's eternal nature.	• Bibles • crepe paper streamer roll • a 12-inch crepe paper streamer piece for every child and you • pens
BUILD ON THE FOUNDATION (about 10 minutes)	***Stream of Life*** Kids will listen to the sound of flowing water as they reflect on God's endless nature.	• portable, tabletop fountain or sound effects of flowing water • pitcher of water • bowl

Before the Lesson

PRESENT THE BIBLE FOUNDATION: *On and On and On*—Tuck one end of a crepe paper streamer roll behind a doorway or window so kids can't see the roll but they can see the end of the streamer sticking out. You need to have a roll long enough that it can go across your room and out another door or window. And prepare your own timeline on crepe paper.

BUILD ON THE FOUNDATION: *Stream of Life*—Borrow a small tabletop or portable recirculating water fountain. If you don't have access to one, use sound effects of running water. Also, pour water into a pitcher and bring along a bowl that's large enough to hold the water in the pitcher.

Ring Around

(about 10 minutes)

Show kids the hula hoop. Form a circle and have kids join hands so two kids have joined hands through the middle of a hula hoop. All kids should have a partner.

SAY:
Let's see if you can pass this hoop around the circle without letting go of your hands. You'll have to be creative!

Let kids pass the hoop around, stepping through it and working together to move the hoop from person to person. Play until everyone has stepped through the hoop and it's back to the kids who started it. Then play the game by draping a jump-rope or 6-foot length of rope over two arms. Ask kids to try to pass the rope around without letting go of hands. (It's next to impossible.) Let kids drop hands and sit down.

ASK:
- **What was challenging about this game?**
- **How was the game different when I put a jump rope over your arms?**
- **What do you think made it easier to pass the hula hoop?**

SAY:
We had fun passing the hoop because our arms were joined together. A hoop or circle has something pretty interesting about it.

Have kids gather around the hula hoop and each put one hand on it.

ASK:
- **Where is the beginning of the circle? the end? How can you tell?**

SAY:
A circle really doesn't have a beginning, middle, or end. It just goes on and on and on, around and around and around; it never stops. Today we'll explore how God is everlasting, too. God has always been, God is now, and God always will be.

33

On and On and On

(about 25 minutes)

SAY:
Before we start, let's try something. I want to see how long you can hold your breath. Ready? Go!
Time kids to see who can hold their breath the longest.

SAY:
Wow! A whole [say the time]. **That's pretty good...but compared to a whole day or a lifetime, it's not much at all. This reminds me of a verse about our lives and God.**
Read aloud Psalm 39:4.

ASK:
• **What does this verse tell us about our lives compared to God?**
• **Why do you think God is everlasting, with no beginning or end, like a circle?**

SAY:
The Bible gives us an idea of how old God is. Check out Revelation 1:8. Hand out Bibles, and read the verse together. Explain that alpha is the first letter in the Greek alphabet, and omega is the last letter.

SAY:
According to this passage, God is everlasting! God existed before everything—God's always been around! God is with us now in [year]. **And God's going to live for eternity—that's forever! Here's another way to look at it. Let's make a timeline to look at what this means.**
Hand each child an approximately 12-inch piece of crepe paper streamer and a pen. At one end, have kids write their birthday. Point out that that's the beginning of their timeline. Kids can add important dates, such as "I got my first bike," "I went to

34

Disneyland," or "my little sister was born." After a few minutes, gather kids together and let them share their timelines. Then hold up your own timeline.

SAY:

This timeline shows that we all have a beginning (point to the place where you wrote your birthday) **and—whether we like it or not—an end.** (Point to the other end of your streamer.) **You and I will each die. But God is everlasting.**

Help kids look up and read 1 Chronicles 16:36 and 1 Timothy 1:17.

ASK:
- **What do these verses tell you about God?**
- **Why does it matter to you that God is everlasting?**

SAY:

It's hard for us to imagine that God didn't have a beginning. I mean, *everything* has a beginning, right? But God's timeline would look more like this.

Pull the end of the crepe paper streamer gently, so the roll stays tucked under the doorway or window. Explain that God's "beginning" is out of our view—we can't see it. Pull the crepe paper gently across the room and out the other door or window. Place this end outside where kids can't see the end any longer.

SAY:

God's "ending" is also out of sight for us. Most things we know of have an ending or they die. But the Bible tells us that God never dies! God is everlasting.

ASK:
- **How would the world be different if God wasn't everlasting?**
- **Why do you think God wants us to know that he's everlasting?**

SAY:

Even though God has been around forever—and has known, created, and cared about everyone from Adam to each baby born today—God still loves you enough to hear every single prayer you pray.

Have kids set their timelines aside.

35

Stream of Life

(about 10 minutes)

Hold up a pitcher of water.

SAY:

Our lives are kind of like this pitcher of water. As I pour the water, call out all the things you love to do. Stop when there's no more water in the pitcher.

Pour the pitcher slowly into the bowl, allowing kids to call out things like "play soccer," "have slumber parties," "text my friends," or "take dance class." When all the water is poured out, have kids stop. Pause for a few seconds of silence.

SAY:

Our lives here on earth will end. But God has promised us eternal life—life forever with him—for those who believe in him.

Turn on the fountain, or play the sound effects of a stream. Ask kids to close their eyes and imagine what eternal life with God might be like.

SAY:

Take a minute to silently pray. Thank God for the promise of a life that goes on and on. Listen quietly for God to encourage you or comfort you as you go through hard things here in your life on earth.

Keep the fountain (or sound effects) going for one full minute. Allow kids to have a quiet, reflective time with God.

After a few moments, lead kids in prayer.

PRAY:

Everlasting God, it's hard for us to understand that you have no beginning and no end. You're such a big, amazing God! But your Word tells us that you still love and care for each of us. Thank you, God! We pray that you'll guide us as we live each day. Help us live in a way that honors you and pleases you. In Jesus' name, amen.

Leave the fountain going as kids leave.

36

Jesus Is Human and Divine

W hat an amazing thing that the fully divine Son of God chose to come to earth in the flesh for our redemption! This essential aspect of the nature of God's Son as both divine and human is one of the most important biblical foundations kids need to understand. We can celebrate year-round the miracle that God chose to become fully human in the form of Jesus to save the world. In this lesson, kids discover that God's Son Jesus came to earth in the flesh.

Scripture Foundation

HEBREWS 2:14-15
God sent Jesus as a human being to break the power of death and sin for us.

LUKE 2:52
Jesus grew as a wise human and in favor with God and people.

THIS LESSON AT A GLANCE

SEQUENCE	EXPERIENCES	SUPPLIES
SET THE FOUNDATION (about 10 minutes)	***Secrets*** Kids will play a game to explore the idea of Jesus coming to earth in the flesh.	• *optional:* CD of soft music, CD player
PRESENT THE BIBLE FOUNDATION (about 25 minutes)	***Jesus in the Flesh*** Kids will explore Hebrews 2:14-15 to better understand why Jesus had to come in the flesh to earth.	• Bibles • colored pencils • a copy of the "Jesus: Hebrews 2:14" handout for each child (p. 43)
BUILD ON THE FOUNDATION (about 10 minutes)	***Birthday Party for Jesus*** Kids will throw a birthday party for Jesus, write a card, and decide what gift they'd bring.	• Bibles • cake, cookies, or cupcakes

Secrets

(about 10 minutes)

SAY:

Today we're going to discover the truth for ourselves that Jesus came to earth in the flesh. Another word for this is *Incarnation*. For a long time Christians have repeated statements each week when they gather for worship. One of those statements, called the Nicene Creed, says: "We believe in one Lord, Jesus Christ, the only Son of God...For us and for our salvation he came down from heaven, was incarnate of the Holy Spirit and the Virgin Mary and became truly human."

Let's play a game together to help us explore the truth that Jesus the Son of God came to earth in the flesh. It's called Secrets.

Form trios. Have one person in each trio act as the Secret-Bearer and go to one side of the room while the other two stay on the opposite side. Tell kids that the goal of Secrets is for the one team member who knows the secret to communicate it with the other two people in the trio. Tell kids that the rules will slightly change with each round of the game.

For the first round, whisper this phrase into the ear of each Secret-Bearer: "God made the world." Give kids a few minutes to pantomime this phrase to the others. If none of the teams is able to guess it, tell them the correct phrase and then have another person from the team come to the other side of the room for round two.

For the next round, tell kids that their Secret-Bearer will be able to whisper the phrase very quietly as they repeat the phrase back word for word. During this round, play soft music in the background or hum or clap or make some sounds that'll make it difficult for teams to hear the whispered phrase. Here's the phrase to tell each Secret-Bearer: "God was sad because people sinned." Give kids a few minutes to play this round. A sense of frustration as they play the first and second round is actually a good thing to help kids understand the emotion behind why Jesus had to come to earth in person.

For the final round, go to each of the remaining Secret-Bearers and whisper this secret phrase: "God sent his Son Jesus for you." Then have the Secret-Bearers walk across the room and tell the secret phrase to their trio members. Ask the teams to repeat in unison this phrase word for word. Congratulate all the teams on a game well played.

39

ASK:

- Why was it hard to communicate your secret when you were across the room?
- Why was it hard to hear the secret when it was whispered by the second person?
- What made it easier to get the secret the last time we played the game?
- How's moving closer to share your secret like or unlike Jesus coming to earth for us?

SAY:

Let's take a deeper look into what it means for Jesus to be God and in the flesh.

PRESENT THE BIBLE FOUNDATION

Jesus in the Flesh

(about 10 minutes)

SAY:

Let's explore together what the Bible says about Jesus coming to earth in the flesh. Have a willing child read aloud Hebrews 2:14-15.

SAY:

Let's create a storyboard that can show our friends and our parents why Jesus came in the flesh to earth. Hand out the "Jesus: Hebrews 2:14" handout page and colored pencils. I'll read the verse and then you'll create a picture in each box that shows that part of this true story from the Bible. Hebrews 2:14 begins by saying, "Because God's children are human beings—made of flesh and blood..." Draw a picture in the first box on the left of your page to represent the people Jesus came for. Give kids a few minutes to complete this drawing. Have them hold up their drawings before you

40

move on to the next box in the storyboard. If the older kids have extra time, they can write the portion of the verse or a paraphrase of it under each panel.

Next our verse from Hebrews says, "The Son also became flesh and blood." Draw a picture of Jesus coming to earth as a baby in the second box above the word *Christmas*. Give kids a few minutes to draw this scene.

The last part of our verse from Hebrews says, "For only as a human being could he die, and only by dying could he break the power of the devil, who had the power of death." Create a drawing in the third box of Jesus dying on the cross. Again allow kids enough time to create this picture.

After kids have had a few minutes to complete their storyboards, ask volunteers to share their creations with the rest of the group. When all who choose to share have finished, continue.

SAY:
Thanks for sharing your artwork! Be sure to share it either at home with your family or with your friends...or both! You've just created your own storyboard that tells the greatest story and the best news of all time.

BUILD ON THE FOUNDATION

Birthday Party for Jesus

(about 10 minutes)

SAY:
One way we show our love for our friends and families is to throw them a birthday party each year to celebrate the day they were born. Let's throw a birthday party right now for our friend Jesus, who was born and lived on earth just as we do. Christmas isn't the only day that we can celebrate that Jesus was born just like we were. Today's a great day to party for Jesus.

41

Let's sing "Happy Birthday" to Jesus and then enjoy the food. Lead the kids in the "Happy Birthday" song, and then serve the food for them to enjoy. After all have had a chance to enjoy the snack, pass out wet wipes to clean hands.

ALLERGY ALERT

See page 8

ASK:

• **When we're invited to birthday parties, we usually bring a gift. If you could pick anything in the world to bring to Jesus, what would you choose?**

Encourage kids to shout out their ideas for birthday gifts for Jesus. Close your time together with this responsive prayer.

SAY:

I'm glad that Jesus, God's Son, came to earth as a real person. As we close our time together, let's act out the process of growing up. Lie down and curl up in a ball. Pretend you're a little baby again. (Pause.) **Go ahead and make baby noises.** (Pause.) **Now slowly move to your knees but stay curled up. Gradually uncurl and stretch your neck up.** (Pause.) **Now slowly stand to your feet.** (Pause.) **Finally stretch your arms up. Good job!**

As our closing prayer, let's do it again and this time I'll read a verse to you about Jesus during his time on earth as a kid.

Please lie down again and curl up in a ball. (Pause.) **Here's what the Bible says in Luke 2:52.**

> **"Jesus grew…" Okay, now gradually uncurl and stretch your neck up.** (Pause.)
> **"Jesus grew in wisdom…" Now slowly stand up.** (Pause.)
> **"Jesus grew in wisdom and in stature…" Stretch your arms up.** (Pause.)
> **"Jesus grew in wisdom and in stature and in favor with God and all the people."**

With their arms stretched up in prayer, ask kids to each thank Jesus for one thing. You go first. When all who wish to have shared, close in prayer.

PRAY:

Thank you, God, for sending Jesus to be here on earth in the flesh with us. Help us every day to grow in friendship with you. In Jesus' name, amen.

JESUS: Hebrews 2:14

Children

Christmas

Cross

LESSON 5: Jesus Is Human and Divine

LESSON 6

Jesus, the Humble King

Pride. Individualism. The desire to be first and best. That's our modern way of life, isn't it? It's certainly the natural way of humankind. But it's not Jesus' way. He's the King of heaven and earth, yet he put others first and lived a human life of deep humility. And our King wants us to follow his example and do the same, which isn't always easy. In this study kids will explore Jesus' humble life and how we can model our actions after his.

Scripture Foundation

LUKE 1:30-33
Jesus is king.

LUKE 2:1-7
Jesus is born in a stable and sleeps in a manger.

PHILIPPIANS 2:3-8
Jesus humbles himself before God and becomes a servant.

THIS LESSON AT A GLANCE

SEQUENCE	EXPERIENCES	SUPPLIES
SET THE FOUNDATION (about 10 minutes)	*Your Chair, Please* Kids will scramble to find the right chair.	• chairs • a die cube • masking tape • marker
PRESENT THE BIBLE FOUNDATION (about 25 minutes)	*Humble Beginnings* Kids will consider Jesus' humble beginnings and draw pictures from Jesus' life.	• Bibles • strips of cotton fabric • soft baby blanket • markers • white paper
BUILD ON THE FOUNDATION (about 10 minutes)	*Crowns of Glory* Kids will lay down a crown of pride, and give an act of humility to Jesus as a gift.	• paper • scissors • tape • pens or pencils • low-tack masking tape • CD of soft, reflective music • CD player

Before the Lesson

SET THE FOUNDATION: *Your Chair, Please*—For every six children you have, set up a row of six chairs. In each row, place six chairs in a straight line facing forward, one chair in front of the other, with enough room for kids to move around. Using tape and a marker, label the chairs 1st, 2nd, 3rd, 4th, 5th, and 6th from front to back.

BUILD ON THE FOUNDATION: *Crowns of Glory*—Using the masking tape, make a large cross on one wall where kids will lay their crowns.

46

Your Chair, Please

(about 10 minutes)

Form a circle.

SAY:

We're going to play a game to see who'll get the best seat. Start by finding a chair. It doesn't matter which chair you choose; you just need a chair to sit in.

Explain that in this game, kids will try to get the best seat—first place in front of the row. The goal of the game is to be in the number one chair when the game ends.

Tell kids that you'll roll the die and then say the number aloud. The child sitting in the corresponding number of chair gets to ask the person in front of him or her to trade places, and that person has to do so. The person in the number one chair can only ask to switch places with the person in the number six chair, though, placing him or her in the back of the row. Let kids know you'll roll the die 10 times and then the game is over.

Roll the die and call out the number. Pause after each roll for kids to switch places. The faster you roll the die, the faster the action.

After 10 rolls, stop.

ASK:

- **What was it like for you to give up your seat to someone who was farther from the first place seat?**

SAY:

We all like to be in first place and win the game. It's difficult to give up a better position or prize to someone else, but that's what Jesus wants us to do. Let's play again, but this time we'll change the goal. When I roll your number, you can ask anyone to trade you places, but your goal this time is to put yourself last and someone else in first place. Let's see how you do.

Play again and see who ends up in last place, or the sixth chair.

47

ASK:
• What was this game like with the new goal?
• What's it like when someone gets first place and you lose?

SAY:
Being first is good. But Jesus wants us to know that being humble and putting others first is actually even better—and that's what he wants us to do. Today we're going to explore humility. Jesus is the humble king even though he has more reason to be proud than anyone. He's a king. And not just any king—he's the King over all kings and King over heaven and earth. Let's grab our Bibles and see what it tells us.

PRESENT THE BIBLE FOUNDATION

Humble Beginnings

(about 25 minutes)

SAY:
We know that Jesus is God's Son. And the Bible also says that he's a king. Let's read Luke 1:30-33.
Lead kids in reading Luke 1:30-33.

ASK:
• What did Jesus have to be proud of?

SAY:
Like other princes, Jesus was born to be a king. Unlike other kings though, God said that Jesus would reign forever. From the beginning, Jesus wasn't like other kings.

48   Lead kids in reading Luke 2:1-7.

ASK:

• What was different about Jesus' birth and your birth?

SAY:

Jesus was born in a barn, wrapped in swaddling clothes, and placed in a feed trough. Not exactly a birth fit for a king.

Distribute strips of cloth. Ask kids to pay attention to how the cloth feels.

SAY:

This is similar to what Jesus was wrapped in as a baby. But remember, Mary and Joseph had been traveling, so it's not like these clothes were fresh from the washing machine and dried with fabric softener.

ASK:

• What would you expect a prince to be wrapped in as a baby?

Pass around the baby blanket.

SAY:

This is what a prince should be wrapped in—something soft and warm. But even from the beginning, Jesus was a different kind of king. He wasn't what the Jewish people expected, and he's not always what we expect either. Let's see how humble Jesus was.

Have kids choose a partner. Give each pair a Bible, a marker, and paper. Assign one of the following Scriptures to each pair. Give kids time to read their passages, and then tell them they may no longer talk to each other. Challenge each pair to work together to draw the scene they just read about. The catch: They must both hold the same marker at the same time to draw—without speaking.

John 13:3-5
Luke 19:28-38
Mark 15:22-32

Allow about 10 minutes for kids to work on their scenes. Then bring kids back together.

ASK:

• What was challenging about drawing your scene?
• In what ways did you and your partner work together?

49

SAY:

It takes humility to let someone else go first and make decisions you might want to make. But that's exactly what Jesus wants us to do—to consider others as important. Let's hear about your pictures.

Have partners read aloud their assigned passage, show their picture, and discuss how Jesus showed humility in the passage.

SAY:

All these examples show us that Jesus put others first and that he wasn't concerned about looking like a king. Let's see why the Bible tells us that's important to us.

Read Philippians 2:6-8.

ASK:

• Why is it important that Jesus chose humility and obedience?

• What would be different for us if Jesus hadn't been humble?

• Why do you think Jesus wants us to follow his example and be humble?

SAY:

Jesus is the humble king. He could've stayed in heaven and not given us a way to be forgiven for our sins. He could've come as a royal king, wearing a gold crown and riding a gallant horse. He could've stayed in a palace, but instead he chose to come as a servant, offering himself as the sacrifice for our sins. How amazing is that? Jesus made the choice to be humble, and he wants us to be humble, too. Let's explore that.

Crowns of Glory

(about 10 minutes)

ASK:
• What do you think it means to be a humble person?

SAY:
Humility isn't easy. We usually look out for ourselves first. We don't naturally put others first or do things that make us uncomfortable. That's called pride, and most of us wear pride like a crown—even if we don't know it. Hand out paper, scissors, and tape. Give kids a few minutes to cut out and fashion a paper crown.

SAY:
As you put on your crown, think of all the ways you're special. Think of all the reasons you deserve to be first or to have the best. Pause, and give a few moments for kids to reflect. But God tells us to be humble like Jesus.
Read aloud Philippians 2:3-5. Give each child a pen or pencil.

ASK:
• What does it mean to have the same attitude as Jesus?
• How can you change your attitude this week to follow Jesus' example?

SAY:
Showing humility can be as simple as giving someone your place in line or not asking for the biggest piece of cake. It could be as hard as making friends with the new kid at school or asking forgiveness for something you've done.
Being humble doesn't mean you're less special; it means you recognize another person's importance. Think for a few minutes about how you can be humble this week and write it on the inside of your crown.

51

Play quiet, reflective music while kids work. After a couple minutes, instruct kids to lay their crowns in front of the cross.

SAY:

Jesus wants us to be humble. He wants us to follow his example—to put others first and to not be troubled by what others think about us. Your humility is like a gift to Jesus and to those around you.

Lead kids in prayer, thanking Jesus for his example of humility and obedience.

LESSON 7

Jesus Has Always Existed

oday's world is full of fakes. Spam infiltrates our email accounts, promising outlandish results from miracle pills and creams. Botox, plastic surgery, and airbrushing give ordinary people extraordinary appearances. Con artists, scams, and Ponzi schemes rob the rich and poor alike. And false gods give false hope and snake-oil security in an insecure world. Thankfully, Jesus is a rock in whom we can put our trust. Jesus is no fly-by-night conjurer, no placebo for the very real ills of our society. Not a counterfeit or a false prophet. Jesus is the one who existed before all things, created all things, and sustains all things. In this lesson, kids will learn to trust Jesus to hold their world together because Jesus has always truly been God.

Scripture Foundation

JOHN 1:1-18
Jesus is God, and he existed in the beginning with God. All things were made through him.

COLOSSIANS 1:15-17
Jesus existed before all things; everything was created through him and for him. Jesus holds creation together.

THIS LESSON AT A GLANCE

SEQUENCE	EXPERIENCES	SUPPLIES
SET THE FOUNDATION (about 10 minutes)	**True or False?** Kids will read a series of statements and have three minutes to determine which are true and which are false.	• a photocopy of the "True or False?" handout for each child (p. 60) • pencils
PRESENT THE BIBLE FOUNDATION (about 25 minutes)	**Trash or Treasure, Earthly or Eternal?** Kids will look at John 1 to find clues about Jesus' eternal value and prepare appraisers' reports to show their findings.	• Bibles • newsprint • markers • tape
BUILD ON THE FOUNDATION (about 15 minutes)	**Holding It All Together** Kids will trust Jesus to hold their world together.	• Bibles • newsprint • sticky notes • markers
BONUS ACTIVITY (10-15 minutes)	**Giving Thanks** Kids will write their own psalms of praise to Jesus.	• Bibles • paper • pencils

True or False?

(about 10 minutes)

Give each child a pencil and a "True or False?" handout. Tell children that they may work on the handout individually or with a partner, but they only have three minutes to complete it.

After three minutes, call time and have kids form a circle.

Review kids' responses to the handout. (Only statements 3, 8, and 10 are true.)

ASK:
• How good were you at spotting the real thing versus fake things?
• How do you know when something is real or not?

SAY:
There are lots of fakes and crazy stories out there. We see things every day that make us question whether they're real or fake—celebrities, products, special offers, you name it. There are even TV shows about how many fake antiques and collectibles are out there and just how valuable the real things are. Religions can be fake, too. But when we find the real thing through Jesus, it's more valuable than gold. How do we know what's real? Today we'll discover that Jesus has always existed, and we'll find other clues about his eternal value.

Trash or Treasure, Earthly or Eternal?

(about 25 minutes)

SAY:

Some people believe that Jesus was a good man, a great teacher, and a prophet, but just a man—not God. They think Jesus was the same as Buddha or Mohammed. They say Jesus was born on earth as a human baby and killed on a cross—and that was that. But how do we know that Jesus was the real deal? How do we know that Jesus was more than just a man, that Jesus was indeed God?

Have children form three groups (a group can be one person). Make sure each group has a Bible, a piece of newsprint, and markers. Assign one group John 1:1-5, another group verses 6-13, and the third group verses 14-18.

SAY:

It's time to call in the experts. In your group, read the passage that I've assigned you. Then go back and read it again, this time looking for clues about Jesus' eternal *value*. What I mean is, look for details in those verses that tell you that Jesus is more than just a man. Write your case on the newsprint, and be prepared to present it to everyone. It's okay to record evidence both for and against Jesus' eternal value. Pretend that you're experts telling someone what their collectible is worth—but Jesus is the collectible!

Give children 5 to 10 minutes to prepare their reports. Then call everyone back together. Have groups tape their newsprint to the wall as they do their presentations. Ask for a volunteer from Group 1 to read aloud John 1:1-5. Then have others from the group present their expert findings, appraising Jesus' eternal value. Thank Group 1 for their work. Repeat with Groups 2 and 3.

ASK:

• After hearing the evidence, what did you learn about Jesus?

- **What was it like to try to figure out whether Jesus is the real deal?**
- **Why do you think it's important to figure out whether Jesus is the real thing or whether a religion is real?**

SAY:

The Bible says clearly that Jesus has always existed. Jesus is God's Son; Jesus is God. Jesus even had a big part to play in creation. Let's check out what that means for us.

BUILD ON THE FOUNDATION

Holding It All Together

(about 15 minutes)

Have children turn in their Bibles to Colossians 1:15-17. Ask for a willing child to read these verses aloud.

ASK:

- **What do these verses say Jesus made?**
- **What does verse 17 say about everything that Jesus made?**

SAY:

These verses really sum it up. Jesus existed before everything else began. Everything was created through him and for him, and Jesus holds all creation together. Wow!

ASK:

- **What do you think these verses mean?**
- **How do you think Jesus feels about his creation?**
- **How do you think he holds it all together?**
- **If Jesus holds the whole universe together, what can he do to hold your world together?**

SAY:

Everything was made by, through, and for Jesus, and he holds the whole universe together. Jesus can hold your world together, too. Jesus doesn't want to be just number one on your list, something you check off every Sunday. Jesus wants to be the glue that holds your life together. He wants to be important in every part of your world. Jesus has always existed and always will.

Draw a circle in the middle of a piece of newsprint, and write "Jesus" inside. Then draw four or five other circles surrounding it, like planets orbiting the sun. Ask kids to name all the parts of their life that are important to them, such as school, friends, family, church, sports, and pets. As they name those things, write each word in a different circle.

SAY:

Jesus is like the sun in your life, touching every part of your life. Jesus wants to be important in every part of your life, and he'll hold your whole world together.

ASK:

- **How can knowing that Jesus always existed help you trust him with every part of your life?**
- **What parts of your life do you need to trust Jesus to hold together for you?**

Give kids sticky notes and markers. Encourage kids to write areas of their lives that they want to entrust to Jesus' care on the sticky notes, and stick them on the newsprint. Ask them to write one concern per sticky note.

SAY:

Jesus has always existed, and he holds the whole world together. This is a lot of stuff here that we want Jesus to hold together for us, but we can trust Jesus with it, because he is God.

Have kids gather around the newsprint and silently read through the sticky notes. Then close your time together with a popcorn prayer by opening the prayer time yourself, and then encouraging others to voice any of the requests on the newsprint, no matter whose they are. Children may "pop in" with prayer whenever there's an opportunity. Close the prayer time yourself, thanking Jesus that he has always existed and that he holds our world together.

Giving Thanks

(10 to 15 minutes)

If you have time, try this activity after your closing prayer. Have children turn in their Bibles to Psalm 65.

SAY:
This is a psalm that thanks God for very specific things. As we read it, pay attention to the things David was so thankful for.

Ask for a willing child to read aloud verses 1-4, another to read verses 5-8, and a third to read verses 9-13.

ASK:
- **If you were going to write a psalm to Jesus based on what we learned today, what things would you thank him for?**

Hand out paper and pencils. Let children work individually or in twos or threes to write their own psalms of praise and thanksgiving to Jesus. Remind them to think about what they learned today from John 1 and Colossians 1. Their psalms don't need to be as long as Psalm 65.

When they're finished, have kids join in a circle to praise Jesus with their psalms. Remind kids that all expressions of praise deserve respect. Ask for willing children to read their psalms aloud. If children are too shy to read their own psalms, ask if you can read their psalms for them. If a child resists, don't press.

SAY:
Jesus deserves our praise because Jesus has always existed and always will exist. Jesus created all things and holds the whole world together. Amen.

True or False?

____ 1. Facebook charges monthly subscription fees to users.

____ 2. The artificial sweetener aspartame has been proven responsible for an epidemic of chickenpox-like symptoms in kids.

____ 3. A man collided with a black bear while riding his bike to work. The bear smacked him off his bicycle, ripped off the back tire of his bike, and then fled into nearby woods.

____ 4. Pepsi has new patriotic cans coming out with pictures of the Empire State Building and the Pledge of Allegiance on them. But Pepsi left off two little words on the Pledge: "Under God." Pepsi said they did not want to offend anyone.

____ 5. Major Hollywood studios have all signed agreements to no longer use actors under age 12 in movies in an effort to reduce the number of adults suffering from complications that often result from fame at too early an age.

____ 6. Patriots quarterback Tom Brady was once a cast member of *The Brady Bunch* television series.

____ 7. Diet Coke paid a fine to print that the soda has "just one calorie" on their cans even though it has much more than that. Coke figured it could make more money by convincing people their product has only one calorie than it would cost to pay the fine.

____ 8. A lucky bargain hunter became a millionaire after finding an original print of the Declaration of Independence in the frame of an old painting he bought for $4 at a flea market.

____ 9. Jesus was a good man, a great teacher and prophet, but just a man.

____ 10. Jesus is God's Son, he has always existed, and he is God.

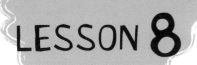

LESSON 8

Jesus Paid for Our Sins

A sk kids how they'd feel about taking the punishment for someone else's wrongdoings...and you'll probably get a resounding, "Are you kidding?" Kids demand fairness, so being punished for someone else's offense is unthinkable. Yet that's exactly what Jesus did for us through his death on the cross. In this lesson, kids will explore just what an unthinkable, unimaginable thing Jesus did for us...and how vast his love truly is!

Scripture Foundation

LEVITICUS 4:1-12
God gives specific instructions about how the Israelites were to make a sin offering.

ROMANS 3:23-25
Paul reminds us that we all sin, but Jesus' sacrifice frees us from the penalty for our sins.

THIS LESSON AT A GLANCE

SEQUENCE	EXPERIENCES	SUPPLIES
SET THE FOUNDATION (about 10 minutes)	***Aim for Perfection*** Kids will aim for a target and pay a penalty if they fall short.	• small, individually wrapped candies such as Starbursts or Life Savers (10 per child) • masking tape • newspaper or newsprint (1 sheet per child)
PRESENT THE BIBLE FOUNDATION (about 25 minutes)	***Sacrificial Lamb*** Kids will use treats to re-create the Israelites' sacrifice and then explore how Jesus became our sacrificial lamb.	• Bibles • pan of brownies or soft, homemade-style cookies • bucket • wet wipes • pitcher of water
BUILD ON THE FOUNDATION (about 10 minutes)	***Gone*** Kids will mark their names on a piece of cloth and then watch as the marks disappear.	• Mark-B-Gone pen (found in the quilting section of most craft or fabric stores or at Amazon.com) • old pillowcases or bedsheets, cut into approximately 6-inch squares • bucket of water

Before the Lesson

SET THE FOUNDATION: *Aim for Perfection* — Use masking tape to make a hand-sized X on one wall. Set a bucket on a table, where everyone has access to it.

When choosing a treat for your "sacrifice," select something absolutely irresistible to kids, such as gooey brownies or doughnuts. The better the treat, the more kids will feel the sacrifice.

62

Aim for Perfection

(about 10 minutes)

SAY:

You're pretty amazing kids! I think you're so amazing that you just might be perfect! But to test you, let's play a game to see just how perfect you are.

Hand each child five pieces of candy and a piece of newspaper or newsprint. Direct kids to wad the newspaper into a ball. Then gather kids at the wall opposite the wall with the X on it. (Kids should be standing about 15 feet away from the X.)

ALLERGY ALERT

See page 8

SAY:

When I say "go," you'll take turns throwing your newspaper ball at the target—that X over there. If you miss the X, you have to give me all your candy.

Play a round, letting each person throw his or her newspaper one time. When everyone has had a turn, have kids retrieve their newspaper wads.

ASK:

- On a scale of 1 to 5, with 1 being "miserable" and 5 being "perfect," how did our group score? Why?
- What was it like to give up your candy?

SAY:

I really like you kids, so I want to give you a second chance. Hand out the candy again. **This time,** [name of a child] **will take all your penalties. Each time someone misses,** [name] **will hand me a piece of his or her candy.**

Play, letting the child you chose pay the penalty for everyone else's mistakes. Then have kids throw away the paper wads.

ASK:

- What did you think when you heard that [name] **would take the penalties for you?**

63

• Tell about a time someone took a punishment for you.

It is best for you as leader to go first when asking kids to tell about a time when someone took a punishment for you. You'll model what you're asking kids to do and give them a moment to think of something to share.

SAY:

This is just a tiny example of what happened for you and me when Jesus died on the cross. Jesus paid for our sins. He took the punishment—which is death—for our wrongdoings. Let's explore the Bible to see why that's such a big deal.

PRESENT THE BIBLE FOUNDATION

Sacrificial Lamb

(about 25 minutes)

Open your Bible to Leviticus 4.

SAY:

In the Bible, the book of Leviticus is full of instructions that God gave the chosen people, the Israelites. God wanted them to live in a way that was different from all the people around them—God wanted them to follow him, to be faithful and to do what's right. But God knew they couldn't be perfect. So…God knew they needed to pay for their wrongdoings— their sins. By doing so, God opened the door for humans to relate more closely to God.

ASK:

• What are some examples of sins?

Allow time for several responses.

64

SAY:

Those are all good examples. According to God's rules in Leviticus, when a person sinned, he or she had to give up something really important.

ASK:

- What's something really important to you that you'd hate to give up?

SAY:

Well, in Bible times, animals were very important—like money is today. Animals like cows, goats, or sheep provided people with food, drink, and clothing. I don't have any cows or goats for you today, but I brought something else.

Bring out the brownies and hand one to each child. Tell kids not to eat the treat.

See page 8

SAY:

When someone sinned, God said that person had to make a sacrifice. In the Bible, that meant taking a bull, a goat, or a lamb to a priest. And it couldn't be an old or sick animal. It had to be a really strong and healthy one—often the best one of the herd. The priest killed the animal in a special ceremony to show a sacrifice of blood. Since the people relied heavily on animals to provide food, fur, and skins, sacrificing an animal was a big cost for people to pay. The people had to trust God in the sacrifice.

Direct kids to bring their brownie "sacrifice" and crumble it into the bucket. Talk about how the priests had a messy job of tending to the sacrifices. Hand kids wet wipes and let them clean up their hands.

SAY:

Then the priest would burn the animal's body. If I burned your sacrifice, we might set off smoke alarms. So we'll destroy it in a different way.

Pour water in the bucket.

ASK:

- How do you think people felt about bringing such valuable things to be sacrificed?
- Why do you think God wanted people to offer sacrifices?

65

SAY:

God loves people so much. And God knew that people couldn't stop sinning. God knew that people would never be perfect. But sin can't be near God because God is holy and perfect. So God made one huge, incredible sacrifice for us.

Help kids look up and read Romans 3:23-25.

ASK:

- How was Jesus like or unlike the cows or goats that the Israelites sacrificed?
- Why do you think God gave up his precious Son, Jesus?

SAY:

Jesus paid for our sins. God took away the punishment for every wrong thing we've ever done—and all the wrong things we'll ever do—when Jesus died on the cross. Because of Jesus, God forgives us and we can live with God forever! Let's spend some time thanking God for his incredible sacrifice of love.

BUILD ON THE FOUNDATION

Gone

(about 10 minutes)

Hand each child a piece of cloth. Have kids scatter around the room and sit on the floor. Set a bucket of clean water in the middle of the room.

SAY:

The book named Romans in the Bible was written by a man named Paul, who really understood what it was like to be forgiven. Paul had really messed up and had some pretty big, awful sins. But listen to what else Paul wrote in Romans 5:8.

66

Read aloud Romans 5:8.

SAY:

God loves you so much, and he sent Jesus to pay for your sins. Because of Jesus' death, your sins can be washed away.

Hand the Mark-B-Gone pen to a child. Explain that kids will take turns writing a sin on their cloth. Assure kids that no one will see what they write—it's between them and God. As kids finish writing, let them crumple their cloth in one fist and hand the pen to another child. When everyone has written, continue.

SAY:

Take a minute to pray about that sin. Ask God to forgive you. Thank God for loving you enough—even when you sin—to send Jesus as a sacrifice who pays for that sin.

After about 30 seconds, direct kids to take turns coming to the bucket of water. Kids will each drop their cloth into the water, swish it around, and then pull it out. Kids can wring out the water and return to their place on the floor. Continue when everyone has had a turn.

ASK:

• **What happened to the sin?**

• **What do you think of what Jesus did to wash away our sins?**

PRAY:

God, thank you for sending Jesus, your chosen Son, to pay for our sins with his life and death. In Jesus' name, amen.

LESSON 9

Jesus Resurrected

hristian kids may've heard more times than they can count that Jesus "died and rose again" or "came back to life." But here's a reality they may not have grappled with: When Jesus' closest friends knew he had died on the cross, they believed it was the end for him—and for them. We can only imagine how their dreams, assumptions, beliefs, and hopes died that day—crushed under the body of their beloved Teacher, hanging on a cruel cross. Worse, all of the disciples deserted Jesus in his hour of greatest need. But God knew the rest of the story! God knew that he would glorify and raise his Son to new life, casting aside the power of sin and changing history…and the eternal future. In this lesson, kids will discover the glory, surprise, meaning, and hope of Jesus' resurrection.

Scripture Foundation

LUKE 24:35-43
Jesus appears to the disciples and eats with them.

MATTHEW 28:8-10, 16-17; MARK 16:9-20; JOHN 20:11-16, 24-28
Jesus appears to his friends after his death.

1 PETER 1:21
Peter explains that God glorified Jesus.

JOHN 11:25
Jesus describes himself as the resurrection.

THIS LESSON AT A GLANCE

SEQUENCE	EXPERIENCES	SUPPLIES
SET THE FOUNDATION (about 10 minutes)	***Surprise!*** Kids get an unexpected surprise and discuss how we react when things don't turn out how we expect.	• large box of raisins • small candy bars
PRESENT THE BIBLE FOUNDATION (about 25 minutes)	***I Don't Believe It*** Kids will search the room for something that ends up being different than what they expect; then they'll explore how Jesus' friends reacted when they saw him alive.	• 4 Bibles • cup of ice • paper • pencils or pens
BUILD ON THE FOUNDATION (about 10 minutes)	***Changed*** Kids compare objects that are the same but look different; then they'll consider how Jesus' resurrection changes us.	• a few raisins • a few grapes • 2 balloons • a few unpopped popcorn kernels • bowl of popcorn • 8- to 8.5-inch square piece of paper with a color or pattern on one side (1 per child)

Before the Lesson

SET THE FOUNDATION: *Surprise!* — Carefully open a box of raisins, take out the raisins, and fill the box with candy bars or another treat. Reseal the box so it appears to never have been opened.

PRESENT THE BIBLE FOUNDATION: *I Don't Believe It* — Bring a cup of ice with you, and set it near your Bible or purse or other personal items. It needs to be where kids see it, but you want them to assume it's just your drink.

BUILD ON THE FOUNDATION: *Changed* — Inflate one balloon; leave the other uninflated. Practice making the paper ball by following the directions on pp. 76-77.

Surprise!

(about 10 minutes)

Welcome kids and have them gather on the floor.

SAY:

I'm so glad to be here today, and I hope that you're excited, too! I'm so happy to see you, because I've brought a surprise to share. Show kids the box of raisins.

See page 8

ASK:

• **What do you think is inside this box? Why? Raise your hand if your favorite treat is raisins.**

Determine which child has on the most blue, and let that child open the box and then hand out what's inside. While kids enjoy their snacks, continue your discussion.

ASK:

• **What was surprising about this snack?**
• **Tell about a time *you* surprised someone.**
• **How do you feel about surprises?**

SAY:

After Jesus died on the cross, his friends were *really* surprised. Things didn't go the way his friends expected when they saw Jesus die on the cross. The big surprise was that Jesus rose from the dead. And now he lives forever!

I Don't Believe It

(about 25 minutes)

SAY:

Before we dig into the Bible, I want you to search for something I've hidden in our room. It's water—that should be pretty easy to find. You've got 30 seconds to find the water. Go!

After 30 seconds (or if a child catches on that your ice is the water), call time and gather kids again. Explain that you were talking about the ice in the cup.

ASK:

• **When I told you to look for water, what did you expect to find?**
• **What did you think when I showed you the ice?**

SAY:

When Jesus died on the cross, his friends thought his life was over—they thought it was the end. They'd followed Jesus, listened to his teachings, seen him do incredible miracles...and they loved him.

ASK:

• **How do you feel about Jesus dying on a cross?**

SAY:

The Bible tells us Jesus came back to life. (Lower your voice.) **But his friends didn't know that was going to happen. Let's see how they reacted when they saw Jesus again.**

Form four groups, and give each group a number from one to four. Hand out Bibles, paper, and pencils or pens, and assign one of the following passages to each group:

Luke 24:35-43
Matthew 28:8-10, 16-17
Mark 16:9-20
John 20:11-16, 24-28

72

SAY:

In your group, work together to read the passage aloud and write your answers to these three questions.

1. What was surprising about the way Jesus appeared to his friends?
2. How did Jesus' friends react when they saw him?
3. Why do you think they did that?

Allow a few minutes for groups to read the passage and record their answers. When everyone is ready, continue.

SAY:

Now, form a new group with one friend from each of the other groups. You'll have a 1, 2, 3, and 4 in your group. Take turns telling what happened in your Scripture passage and how your group answered the questions.

Allow time for kids to form groups and share what they learned. When kids have all had a chance to talk, continue.

ASK:

- What may have made it difficult for Jesus' friends to believe it was him?
- Why is it important that Jesus visited his friends after he died on the cross?

SAY:

There's another passage that tells us something that happened to Jesus after he died.

Read aloud 1 Peter 1:21.

ASK:

- What do you think it means when this passage talks about God giving Jesus "glory"?
- How do you think Jesus looked after he died and came back to life?

SAY:

We don't know whether Jesus looked the same or different. We do read that his friends didn't recognize him. That might be because they didn't expect to see him alive or because there was something different

73

about him. God glorified Jesus—he raised him up from the dead and gave him a new, whole, perfect body. Amazing! Jesus rose from the dead. He died for us, but came to life again through God's power. Jesus is *our* resurrection, because through him we can have life forever!

BUILD ON THE FOUNDATION

Changed

(about 10 minutes)

Set out the grapes and raisins together, the balloons side by side, and the popcorn (both popped and unpopped) together.

ALLERGY
ALERT

ASK:
• **What do you notice about these pairs?**

BALLOON
WARNING

See page 8

SAY:
These pairs are the same things—grapes, balloons, and popcorn. But they look very different. Somehow, they've changed. Think about Jesus before his death and resurrection and Jesus *after* his death and resurrection.

ASK:
• **How was Jesus the same?**
• **How was he different?**
• **What made the difference?**

SAY:
Jesus' resurrection changes us, too! Listen to these words from Jesus—not too long before he died.
Read aloud John 11:25.

ASK:

• **According to this verse, how does Jesus' resurrection change us?**

• **How does knowing Jesus change the way you live every day?**

Hand kids each a square piece of paper. Let kids take a minute to write a prayer on the back of their papers, thanking God for raising Jesus and giving us the chance to have new life, too. Then lead kids in folding their papers according to the directions on pp. 76-77 to make a paper ball. Talk about how the paper has transformed into a ball, as a reminder of the way Jesus' resurrection can change our lives forever.

Paper Ball Instructions

1. You will need an 8- to 8.5-inch square piece of paper with a color and/or pattern on one side and white on the other. Place the paper on a hard surface, color side down. Fold it in half, corner to corner, like a taco. Crease and unfold, keeping the white side up.

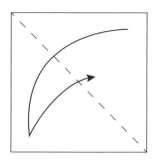

2. Repeat the fold in step 1 using the opposite corners. Crease and unfold. The creases should form an "X" on your paper.

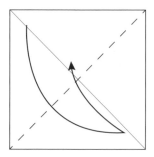

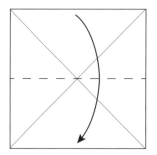

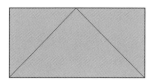

3. Fold the paper in half like a hot dog bun by taking the top edge to the bottom edge. Crease well.

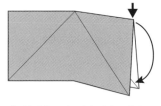

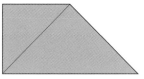

4. Holding the left side of the paper down flat, push the right folded edge down and in so that it tucks into the center. Flatten. Repeat with the left folded edge, forming a triangle.

5. Taking the bottom right point of the top layer triangle only, bring it up to the top point of the triangle. Crease. Repeat with the left side. You should have a diamond shape on top now.

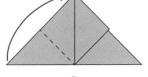

6. Taking the right point of the diamond, fold it in to the center line. Crease. Repeat with the left point of the diamond.

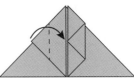

7. Notice that the folds you made in Step 6 created two pockets. Just above and behind the pocket is a triangular flap of paper. Fold that flap into a smaller triangle that will fit inside the pocket, then tuck it into the pocket as far as you can. Do this for both sides.

POCKETS

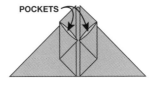

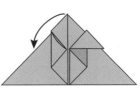

POCKET

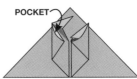

8. Turn the origami over. Repeat Steps 5, 6, and 7 on the other side, forming this shape:

9. One end of the origami has a small opening or hole. Rotate the paper so that the hole is at the top.

HOLE

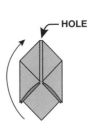

10. Place your index fingers between the flaps on either side, partially unfolding the origami. Blow gently into the hole.

HOLE

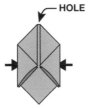

11. The origami expands and you've made a paper ball!

77

LESSON 10

The Holy Spirit Guides and Teaches

Making good decisions is tough. How do we know what to believe, who to trust, which choice will be the right one? The world is often like a jungle, a complex place for even the most experienced of us—let alone for a child. Pressures from school, friends, family, and our culture pull kids in opposing directions. Wouldn't it be great to have a wise and caring guide to lead us through all of life's unknowns? Thankfully, Jesus left us with just such a guide. The Holy Spirit shepherds us toward truth and reminds us of what Jesus taught. Through this lesson kids will learn about and seek the Holy Spirit's guidance toward truth. We could ask for no better guide in life!

Scripture Foundation

JOHN 14:25-26
The Holy Spirit teaches us and reminds us of Jesus' teachings.

JOHN 16:5-15
The Holy Spirit convinces us of sin, righteousness, and judgment. The Holy Spirit guides us to the truth.

THIS LESSON AT A GLANCE

SEQUENCE	EXPERIENCES	SUPPLIES
SET THE FOUNDATION (about 10 minutes)	**Trust Walk** Kids take turns guiding a partner and being guided while blindfolded.	• blindfolds
PRESENT THE BIBLE FOUNDATION (about 25 minutes)	**Teach Me** Kids teach a partner to do a task.	• Bibles • blindfolds • several tennis balls • several paper lunch bags • a few oversized shirts • chairs • paper • pencils
BUILD ON THE FOUNDATION (about 10 minutes)	**Asking for Guidance** Kids write letters asking the Holy Spirit for guidance.	• Bibles • pencils • paper
BONUS ACTIVITY (10-15 minutes)	**Listen** Kids will quietly listen for God.	• none

Before the Lesson

SET THE FOUNDATION: *Trust Walk* — Set up a simple obstacle course in or near your meeting space. This should be something safe for children to complete while blindfolded and walking backward. You'll also one blindfold for every two children.

PRESENT THE BIBLE FOUNDATION: *Teach Me* — Set up the following stations around your meeting space. Station 1: a few sets of tennis or similar balls and paper bags. Station 2: a few oversized shirts. Station 3: a few chairs. Station 4: paper and pencils. You'll also need clean blindfolds, enough for half the children to use at a time.

Leave instructions at each station. At Station 1: "Place a tennis ball into a bag. Then take it back out." At Station 2: "Put on a shirt. Then take it off." At Station 3: "Sit down on a chair." At Station 4: "Draw a picture of a house."

Trust Walk

(about 10 minutes)

Gather kids near the obstacle course you set up before the lesson.

Have children form pairs. Distribute one blindfold per pair. Tell kids that one child will wear the blindfold and walk backward while the other partner guides him or her. Have pairs navigate through the obstacle course, with each guiding partner holding the blindfolded partner's arm to carefully help the person through the obstacle course. The guiding partner must keep the blindfolded partner safe. Kids can use words and their hands to guide their partners.

Once partners make it through the course, have kids switch roles so everyone can guide and be guided through the course.

Form a circle and discuss these questions.

ASK:
- **What was it like to be blindfolded and walk backward through an unknown path?**
- **What was it like to guide your partner through the course?**
- **How was this experience like times in life when you're unsure of what to do?**
- **How was your guide like having the Holy Spirit to guide you?**

SAY:
Sometimes life can be confusing. We might feel confused about what to do or who to listen to. Sometimes we don't even know what the truth is. Thankfully, Jesus sent us the Holy Spirit. The Holy Spirit guides us and teaches us the truth.

Teach Me

(about 25 minutes)

Have children form pairs. Have one child in each pair put on a blindfold.

SAY:

You and your partner are going to go around the room and do some easy tasks together. The guide partner will silently read the instructions at each station and then guide the blindfolded partner in doing the task. The catch is, the guide can't speak. You have to use your hands to show your blindfolded partner how to do the task at each station—and you can't just do the task for him or her.

Equally distribute pairs to begin at each of the stations you created before the lesson. Explain that you'll signal for them to move to the next station.

When everyone is finished with each of the stations, gather the children together to discuss the following questions.

ASK:

- **How did your partner guide you through the tasks?**
- **Why do you think God gives us the Holy Spirit to guide us through what we don't know or can't see?**

SAY:

Let's read John 14:25-26. These verses tell us what the Holy Spirit does for us. Read the passage with kids.

SAY:

The Holy Spirit teaches us, guides us, and reminds us of Jesus' teachings. There's no better teacher or helper we could ask for.

God knows that sometimes life can be confusing. We might not know what to do or who to listen to. Sometimes we feel lost or unprepared for what's happening. That's why Jesus sent the Holy Spirit to be with us in his place, to walk beside us and guide us, to be our teacher and our advisor. The Holy Spirit guides us and teaches us the truth.

Asking for Guidance

(about 10 minutes)

Have children turn to John 16:5-15 in their Bibles. Ask for a willing child to read these verses aloud.

ASK:
- **Talk about a time that you've experienced the Holy Spirit guiding you.** Be prepared to start with an example of your own.

SAY:
We can ask the Holy Spirit for help with our questions and problems, and he'll guide us to the truth, reminding us of everything Jesus taught and helping us make good decisions. We won't get a text message back from the Holy Spirit, but he might speak to us through the Bible, through other people, through our prayers, or some other way. Let's spend a few minutes right now writing messages to the Holy Spirit, asking for guidance with our needs.

Distribute paper and pencils so children can each write or draw a message asking the Holy Spirit for guidance in some particular area of their lives. Encourage kids to be specific, and let them move to different parts of your room for privacy if they wish.

After a few minutes, have children find their original partners from the "Teach Me" activity.

SAY:
Everyone has something they need help figuring out. We all need the Holy Spirit to guide us and teach us. Please share with your partner what you drew or wrote on your paper. You don't have to get into a lot of details, but give your friend an idea of how you'd like help. Then spend a few minutes praying for each other, asking the Holy Spirit to guide your partner and show your partner the truth.

Give kids five minutes; then gather them to close.

83

SAY:

Jesus loves us so much that, even though he knew he'd no longer be with us on earth, he wanted us to have a teacher and guide to be with us through our lives. Whenever we feel challenged, confused, sad, or lost, or we just need advice, we can turn to the Holy Spirit and ask God for guidance. The Holy Spirit is always with us, always there to guide us and help us see the truth. Let's pray.

PRAY:

Dear God, thank you for the Holy Spirit and for making sure we're never alone. There are times we feel lost and confused in this life; please help us remember we can turn to you for help any time. In Jesus' name, amen.

Listen

(10 to 15 minutes)

If you have time, try this activity after "Asking for Guidance."

ASK:
- When have you prayed to God for help or advice?
- When have you stopped just to listen for God's answer or to hear what God has to say to you?

SAY:
For most of us, prayer means talking to God. But most of us don't ever stop long enough to listen for God's voice. Let's try that today. I want everyone to find a place where you can get comfortable and not be able to reach another person. Close your eyes and clear your minds. I'll read a Bible verse aloud. Then we'll all be quiet for five minutes, until I give the signal. Concentrate on a word or two from the Bible verse or just on God. And just listen. Listen for anything the Holy Spirit might be saying to you.

When kids are settled, read aloud John 15:26 and the first part of John 16:13, slowly and clearly. Then join the children in the quiet time. After five minutes, call everyone back together.

ASK:
- What surprised you about your quiet time?
- What did you hear from the Holy Spirit?
- How would listening for God as well as talking to him change your prayer times?

SAY:
We don't always hear the Holy Spirit speak to us. Often he will speak to us through the Bible or through other people and sometimes in other ways. But it's important that when we pray to God for advice, we listen for his answer.

85

LESSON 11

The Holy Spirit Helps and Prays for Us

I f you say the words "Holy Spirit" to kids, you may conjure images of something straight out of a Harry Potter movie. Kids, especially younger ones, don't necessarily grasp the difference between the Spirit of the Lord and a ghost they see on television. But the Holy Spirit is one of the greatest blessings God has given us—a loving advocate and intercessor who pleads on our behalf. This lesson will help kids understand what it means to have an advocate (someone who'll go to bat for them) and an intercessor (someone who'll take our needs to God). Once kids are equipped with this knowledge, their understanding of God's power is multiplied.

Scripture Foundation

ROMANS 8:26
The Holy Spirit helps us by praying when we don't know what to pray.

1 JOHN 2:1
The Holy Spirit talks to God on our behalf.

THIS LESSON AT A GLANCE

SEQUENCE	EXPERIENCES	SUPPLIES
SET THE FOUNDATION (about 10 minutes)	**Hot Air Helper** Kids will attempt to inflate and tie 10 balloons in one minute.	• 30 balloons • timer • air or balloon pump (available at party supply stores or at Amazon.com)
PRESENT THE BIBLE FOUNDATION (about 25 minutes)	**Backpack Burden** Kids are faced with one child attempting to carry a heavy load all alone.	• Bibles • backpack • numerous heavy objects (dumbbells, weights, thick books, rocks, and so on) • masking tape • marker
BUILD ON THE FOUNDATION (about 10 minutes)	**Miscommuni-can** Kids will attempt to communicate using two cans, and then try again with a string connection.	• 2 empty, clean cans • 2 empty, clean cans with a hole in the center bottom • a 15-foot length of string

Before the Lesson

PRESENT THE BIBLE FOUNDATION: *Backpack Burden* —Label each heavy object with the masking tape and marker. Write the words *fear, worry, sadness, anger,* and *loneliness,* along with other words with similar meanings. Prepare the backpack by filling it with the heavy objects.

BUILD ON THE FOUNDATION: *Miscommuni-can* —Drill or punch a hole in the center bottom of two of the cans, and string the length of string between them. Tie a thick knot on both ends so the string won't pull free from the cans.

You'll also need two cans without holes in the bottom.

88

Hot Air Helper

(about 10 minutes)

Tell kids you've got a big challenge for them: You're going to give three of them one minute to each inflate and tie off 10 balloons. Ask for three volunteers. Tell them you know it's going to be a challenge, but you're sure they can do it. Start the timer and give them one minute to inflate the balloons. It's highly unlikely any of the kids will be successful. (If they are, they must have superpowers!)

BALLOON WARNING
See page 8

When the timer's gone off and they've all caught their breath, continue.

ASK:
- **How did this challenge seem impossible?**
- **Tell about a time you had to do something that seemed impossible.**
- **What's something that would've made your impossible situation easier?**

SAY:
The great news is that God doesn't expect us to handle every challenge that comes our way all alone. God gave us the Holy Spirit to help us rise to the challenge of difficult situations. In other words, God's given us a "balloon pump"—the Holy Spirit. Pull out your balloon pump. **And help in tying the balloons.** Have two assistants stand beside you. **The right tools change the challenge of inflating these balloons from impossible to possible.**

Set the timer and use the balloon pump and your assistants to inflate and tie the balloons, 10 in one minute.

SAY:
And now what seemed impossible was possible. The Holy Spirit isn't some magical creature that'll make your problems disappear. The Holy Spirit is God as our helper and friend who can teach you and make the difficult challenges in your life a whole lot easier—like the balloon pump did.

89

Backpack Burden

(about 25 minutes)

Have one child come to the front of the group, and ask him or her to pick up the backpack and put it on. It should be heavy enough to make this really difficult.

SAY:

I need you to carry this for me; can you do that? Allow the child to answer. **I was hoping you could carry it for the rest of our time together.** Then turn your attention to the rest of the group while the child with the backpack stands beside you.

ASK:

- **Let's talk about things that weigh us down. What are things that make life harder for kids your age?** After kids name a few things, turn to the backpack child.

ASK:

- **Is that backpack getting heavy?** Allow the child to answer. **Let's see what's inside.** Pull out the item marked *fear.*

SAY:

Hmmm. This big item says "fear" on it. What are things kids have to be afraid of? Allow kids to respond. Pull out another item—this one marked *worry.*

SAY:

What do you worry about? Allow kids to respond.

Repeat this process as you pull out the rest of the items, marked *sadness, loneliness,* and *anger.*

SAY:

Sometimes we feel these things. We feel sad or lonely or mad. Sometimes we're so afraid or worried about something, we don't even know how to pray about it. That's why God gave us the Holy Spirit. The Bible

says the Holy Spirit prays *for* us. He's an intercessor, or someone who prays on our behalf. Let's look at what *intercessor* means.

Let's read Romans 8:26. Help the kids find the verse in their Bibles, and have a willing child read it aloud.

SAY:

The Holy Spirit comes to our aid. The Holy Spirit has all of the right words when we don't have any. Start putting the items back in the backpack. **We try to carry everything on our own, but God gave us the gift of the Holy Spirit so we wouldn't have to.** When the backpack is full, give each child a chance to try to lift it. Then have an adult come forward, put on the backpack, and then stay near the group.

SAY:

This is what the Holy Spirit does for you. The Holy Spirit takes the troubles you have and lets God know about them. Then he says, "Here, let me help you with that" and walks right by our side, carrying the weight.

Have the kids form groups of three or four and discuss the following questions.

ASK:

- **Talk about a time you really needed help—but you didn't get any.**
- **Talk about a time you really needed help—and someone helped you.**
- **Why do you think God wants us to rely on the Holy Spirit and let him carry our troubles?**

Miscommuni-can

(about 10 minutes)

ASK:
• Based on what we've talked about so far, what do you think it means to be an intercessor?

SAY:
Let's see if we can figure out exactly what an intercessor is. The Bible tells us that the Holy Spirit is an intercessor for us, so it's important to know what that means.

Have kids form a line against one wall with the child in front holding an empty can (not connected by string). You'll stand on the opposite side of the room with the other empty can. Instruct the child in the front of the line to take three steps away from the line and then put the can to his or her ear to listen to what you're about to say. When the child is ready, quietly say, "The Holy Spirit intercedes for us." Then have the child pass the can, and repeat the experience until each child has had a turn.

ASK:
• Okay, what did I say?
Kids probably won't be able to answer. Tell the group what you said.

ASK:
• Why couldn't you hear my message?
• How do you think God is able to hear you when you talk to him?

SAY:
Sometimes it feels like our prayers are only tiny whispers to God, and we wonder how he could possibly hear us. Sometimes we pray and pray but it doesn't feel like anyone's listening. The good news is that the Holy Spirit intercedes for us. Now, what in the world does *intercede* mean? Well, *inter* means "between" and *cede* means "to go." The Holy Spirit goes *between* God and us. The Holy Spirit speaks for us and talks to

92

God for us when we don't have all the right things to say.

Let's try this again. Change the cans for the ones with the string, and have the kids again form a line on one side of the room. Give the first child in line one can. You stand across the room so the string is tight between you. Then say, "The Holy Spirit goes between God and us." Repeat the action until each child has had a chance to listen. This time, the kids will hear you. When you're done, have everyone say the sentence with you.

SAY:

This string is just like the Holy Spirit. The Holy Spirit helps our prayers to be heard and makes communication with God easier. We're so fortunate to have the Holy Spirit on our side!

ASK:

- Tell about a time you knew God heard your prayer.
- Why do you think God gave us the Holy Spirit to help get our messages to God?

PRAY:

Let's pray now as we close our time together, knowing that the Holy Spirit will help our messages along.

Dear God, we are so thankful for the Holy Spirit. We know how important it is to have someone on our side to help us talk to you and make our load a little bit lighter. Thank you for watching over us. Please help us remember to rely on your Spirit every single day. In Jesus' name, amen.

The Holy Spirit Is Everywhere

The Holy Spirit is present, both inside us and on earth with us. The very idea of who the Holy Spirit is and how the Holy Spirit can be in more than one place at a time is confusing. Yet understanding the presence of the Holy Spirit is essential to children's spiritual growth. When kids learn that something doesn't have to be visible to be real and they grasp why God gave us the Holy Spirit, they see how he fits into their lives.

Scripture Foundation

ROMANS 8:11
The same Spirit that raised Jesus from death gives us life.

JOHN 14:16-17
Jesus promises his disciples that God will give them the gift of the Holy Spirit.

GALATIANS 5:22-23
Paul names the fruit of the Spirit.

THIS LESSON AT A GLANCE

SEQUENCE	EXPERIENCES	SUPPLIES
SET THE FOUNDATION (about 10 minutes)	**Holy Spirit Breath** Kids will move the cotton balls by blowing into the straws, making the point that what's unseen is still powerful.	• cotton balls • straws
PRESENT THE BIBLE FOUNDATION (about 25 minutes)	**Silly Dough Trio** Kids will make putty dough using three ingredients, which will each become unrecognizable though still present.	• Bibles • 1 cup of Elmer's white glue per group of 4 kids • ¾ cup of warm water per group • ½ tsp of Borax per group • 1 bowl per group • 1 large spoon per group
BUILD ON THE FOUNDATION (about 10 minutes)	**Juicy Fruit** Kids will sort through several scenarios to determine which fruit of the Spirit would be at work to resolve them well.	• Bibles • images of strawberries, bananas, oranges, kiwis, grapes, pineapples, apples, peaches, lemons (each child will need one fruit image)

Holy Spirit Breath

(about 10 minutes)

Welcome kids warmly and ask how their week went.

SAY:

Let's start with a big question: What do you think of when I say the words *Holy Spirit*? Allow time for kids to respond. **We know Jesus rose from the dead, but he knew he wouldn't stay on earth forever—his place was in heaven. But Jesus didn't want to leave us on our own, so when Jesus was on his way to heaven, the Holy Spirit came to earth. And now he lives inside of every person who believes in Jesus.**

Have the kids move to one side of the room. Give each child a cotton ball and a straw.

SAY:

Here's your challenge: Put your cotton ball on the floor, and blow it all the way over to the other side of the room—without ever touching it with your hands or with the straw. You've got one minute. Ready?

Give the kids time to move their cotton from one side to the other. Afterward, gather them together.

SAY:

I didn't see anything coming out of your straws, but you could still move the cotton all the way to the other side of the room.

ASK:

- **How can something you can't see have the power to move something else?**
- **How is the air from your straw like the Holy Spirit?**

SAY:

Even though you can't see the Holy Spirit, you can experience his power. Sometimes you can feel the Holy Spirit's work inside you, and

sometimes you can see the power of the Holy Spirit around you. Just as the cotton moved because of an unseen force, we feel the impact of the unseen Holy Spirit. Let's see what the Bible tells us about how the Holy Spirit is everywhere.

PRESENT THE BIBLE FOUNDATION

Silly Dough Trio

(about 25 minutes)

SAY:
One of the coolest things about God is that God knew we'd need help at times, but that sometimes we forget to ask. The Holy Spirit is everywhere, both in us and on earth. But you can't look in the mirror and see the Holy Spirit. It may be easy to forget the Holy Spirit is even there because we don't see him.

Ask for willing children to read aloud Romans 8:11 and John 14:16-17.

SAY:
These words from the Bible promise that the Holy Spirit will live in us. But how is it possible to have something inside you that you can't see? You can see every other part of your body, right? Let's try an experiment that might help us understand a little better. We're going to make silly dough right now.

Have kids form groups of four or fewer. Give each group a set of ingredients and a bowl.

SAY:
Let's start by mixing all our ingredients together. First, pour in the **glue.** Have one person in each group pour the glue into the bowl. Then add the other ingredients, one at a time. Instruct kids to mix them, and then show them how to knead the mixture well. Once the mixture is pliable, let kids each have a piece to play

98

with for a few minutes. Tell them to try to create something that looks like their version of the Holy Spirit.

ASK:
- **Where is the glue now? the water? the Borax powder?**
- **Why do you think you can't see the individual ingredients?**
- **How are the ingredients in the dough like or unlike how the Holy Spirit lives in each of us?**

SAY:
Even though the separate ingredients aren't visible, we *know* they're still in your silly dough. It's the same for us. Once we get with Jesus, choosing to believe in and follow him, the Holy Spirit is within us. We'll never be the same, just as the individual ingredients won't be the same. But we'll be much, much more. Let's look at ways you might see the Holy Spirit in your life.

BUILD ON THE FOUNDATION

Juicy Fruit

(about 10 minutes)

SAY:
Once the Holy Spirit lives inside us, he changes us. The Bible describes nine different things that prove the Holy Spirit is working in our lives. They're called fruit of the Spirit. Let's take a closer look at each one.

Ask for a willing child to read Galatians 5:22-23.

SAY:
Now that we know what the fruit of the Spirit is, each of you is going to get a different fruit. Each fruit represents a fruit of the Spirit—the

things in our lives that show the world the Holy Spirit lives inside us.

Hand out one fruit image per child. Write what each fruit represents where all kids can see; then expand briefly on what each fruit of the Spirit means.

Love: Strawberries

Joy: Banana

Peace: Orange

Patience: Kiwi

Kindness: Grapes

Goodness: Pineapple

Faithfulness: Apple

Gentleness: Peach

Self-Control: Lemon

SAY:

I'm going to read you some situations. Your job is to hold up your fruit picture if you think the person in the situation needs your fruit.

Read the following scenarios, and ask how kids would show their fruit of the Spirit in each situation.

ASK:

• How would you show your fruit of the Spirit in this situation?

My mom said I could go over to my friend's house today, but only after she gets groceries and runs her errands. It's taking a really long time, and I just want to hurry up and get there!

I have piano lessons every Wednesday after school. I don't want to go, but I know the teacher is counting on me to show up and practice for our recital.

We're having dinner in 15 minutes, but I don't want meatloaf. I want the candy bar I saw sitting on the counter. My parents said I have to wait to have it, but I don't think they'd even notice if I took a bite or two.

There's a new kid at our school. He's sitting at the table next to mine at lunch, but he's all by himself.

ASK:

• Why is it important to have the fruit of the Spirit in your life?

• Which of these fruits is hardest for you to show, and why?

SAY:

You've been a great bunch today! Now let's close in prayer.

PRAY:

Dear God, thank you for sending the Holy Spirit to live inside of us. Help us always make good choices to show the Spirit working in our lives. In Jesus' name, amen.

The Holy Spirit Is a Gift Giver

The Holy Spirit gives us gifts and helps us figure out how to use them. Christmas morning is filled with wonder and anticipation—often accompanied by a pile of presents under the tree. Those gifts have kids' fingers itching before the sun even rises. Everyone loves presents—and gifts from our Creator outshine the best gifts we've ever received. In this lesson, kids will learn that God loves them so much—and so personally—that he gave them each unique gifts through the Holy Spirit. And as a bonus, he gave them all the tools they need to use those gifts.

Scripture Foundation

1 CORINTHIANS 12:4-11
The Holy Spirit gives an abundance of unique gifts; there is only one Spirit.

THIS LESSON AT A GLANCE

SEQUENCE	EXPERIENCES	SUPPLIES
SET THE FOUNDATION (about 10 minutes)	**Tools of the Trade** Kids will perform tasks—but they won't have proper tools to do so.	• large poster board, cut into pieces like a puzzle • ruler • string • bag of cotton • sheet of paper with several hearts on it • bin or box marked "Holy Spirit" with the following items inside: roll of tape, small bag of party decorations (such as party hat, noisemaker, streamers), scissors
PRESENT THE BIBLE FOUNDATION (about 25 minutes)	**Mix & Match** Kids will look at spiritual gifts and identify their own.	• Bible • 6 sets of spiritual gift cards (pp. 108-109)
BUILD ON THE FOUNDATION (about 10 minutes)	**Act It Out!** Kids will act out scenarios to help them uncover some of the gifts God's given them.	• none

Before the Lesson

PRESENT THE BIBLE FOUNDATION: *Mix & Match*—Make double-sided copies of the spiritual gift cards and cut them out, stacking them with the description facing up. On the back is the name and definition of the spiritual gift that's described on the other side. Make six copies of each.

104

Tools of the Trade

(about 10 minutes)

Have kids form three groups.

SAY:
I have some tasks to do and I need a little help. Don't worry, these are simple tasks—anyone could do them.
Hand the first group the poster board puzzle. Tell them their task is to put the puzzle together and hang it on the wall. If they ask questions, just smile at them and tell them you know they can figure it out.

Go to the next group and have them choose one random person as the "birthday boy or girl." Then explain that while they can't decorate the entire room for a celebration, they can decorate the child. Hand the group a ruler, some string, and a bag of cotton; then walk away.

Hand the third group a piece of paper with several hearts on it. Tell kids their task is to cut out all the hearts from the paper.

SAY:
Let's get started! Let's see which group can accomplish its task first. Ready? Go! The kids may attempt to do what you've asked, but they'll be unable to meet their goal. Respond to their questions with a smile as if you have no idea why the challenge is so difficult for them. After 30 seconds, look around expectantly.

ASK:
• **Why aren't you finished yet? It's been almost a minute!...What's wrong? Why couldn't you finish your task?**

SAY:
It sounds like you might need a few more tools to do what I've asked. Go to Group 1.

105

ASK:

- **What would make your job easier?** After they answer, pull a roll of tape from the covered bin marked "Holy Spirit." Go to Group 2.

ASK:

- **What would make your job easier? After they respond, pull out a bag full of party decorations (noisemaker, streamers, party hat). Go to Group 3.**

ASK:

- **How about you? Do you need something to finish your job?** After they answer, give them the scissors.

Give groups a minute to see if they can complete their tasks. Then form a circle.

ASK:

- **Tell about a time you couldn't do something because you didn't have the right tool.**
- **How is having the right tools for a job similar to having the right tools in life?**
- **Why do you think God gives us each specific tools or gifts?**

SAY:

God won't ask us to do a job without giving us the tools to do it. He only asks us to do what he's given us the tools to tackle. Some of these tools are called gifts of the Holy Spirit. Ask for a willing child to read 1 Corinthians 12:4-11.

SAY:

Let's take a look at these tools or gifts and find out more about what the Holy Spirit has given you.

Mix & Match

(about 25 minutes)

Have kids sit in a circle. Place the stack of cards with kid-friendly definitions of spiritual gifts near you on the floor.

SAY:

If you think about it, it's truly awesome that the Holy Spirit has given us each specific gifts to use in our lives. Everyone's gifts are different and special. And the Holy Spirit knows each of us so well that he gave us exactly the gifts we need. Let's take a look at some of the gifts in our circle right now.

Here I have 14 cards. I'm going to read what each card says. I want you to think about each description, and if you know it fits you really well, stand up and then sit down. If you feel like more than one gift describes you, that's fine. Just stand again.

One by one, read the "description" side of the cards aloud to the kids. Allow time for kids to think about the description and for a few to stand. Once kids are standing, turn over the card and read the gift and its definition. Give kids who stood a copy of that card to take home. Then have kids sit down, and move on to the next card. Once you've read through all of the cards, have kids form groups of two or three to discuss the following questions.

ASK:

- **When have you used one of your gifts from God?**
- **In what ways can you use your gifts in the future?**
- **Why do you think the Holy Spirit gave you these specific gifts?**

Spiritual Gift Cards

Side 1: Description

1.	2.	3.	4.	5.
You love to help other people any way you can— even if you don't get credit for it.	When you pray, you know God talks to you, even telling you things you want to tell other people.	When you read the Bible, it makes sense. People say you've got common sense.	In your heart, you know God will always come through. You have no doubts that he answers your prayers.	You pray for people, and they get better.
6.	**7.**	**8.**	**9.**	**10.**
You can tell when someone doesn't understand something, and you can put it in a way that makes sense to that person.	You don't make a big deal out of other people's mistakes.	You've seen God do amazing things through you.	You feel comfortable being in charge. Your friends want to know what you think before they do something.	You aren't selfish. You give freely of everything you have—to best friends *and* to strangers.
11.	**12.**	**13.**	**14.**	
People tell you you're smart. You seem to have the right answers when others are unsure.	You don't hold grudges. When people say they're sorry, you forget they ever hurt you and don't bring it up again.	You know what's right and what's wrong. You know what's true and what's false.	You love encouraging others. You praise others and congratulate people who get awards and recognition.	

13 Most Important Bible Lessons For Kids About God

Spiritual Gift Cards

Side 2: Gift and Definition

5.	4.	3.	2.	1.
Gift: Healing	**Gift: Faith**	**Gift: Wisdom**	**Gift: Prophecy**	**Gift: Service**
curing and making well	confidence and trust in God	knowledge and good judgment	future insight	helping others
10.	**9.**	**8.**	**7.**	**6.**
Gift: Giving	**Gift: Leadership**	**Gift: Miraculous Powers**	**Gift: Mercy**	**Gift: Teaching**
warmth and generosity	guiding and directing	amazing abilities	compassion	transferring knowledge and understanding
	14.	**13.**	**12.**	**11.**
	Gift: Exhortation	**Gift: Discernment**	**Gift: Forgiveness**	**Gift: Knowledge**
	encouraging and advocating	awareness	grace and charity	intelligence

LESSON 13: The Holy Spirit Is a Gift Giver

Act It Out!

(about 10 minutes)

SAY:

God gave each of us gifts that we can use every day; in fact, sometimes we use those gifts and don't even realize it. Let's act out a few scenarios and look for ways you can use your specific gifts in each scenario.

Ask for willing kids to come up and act out each of the following scenarios.

> *An older brother who doesn't want to share with his little brother.*
>
> *A child crying on the playground.*
>
> *A friend who's upset about a mean email she got from someone she thought was her friend.*
>
> *A friend who comes up to you to apologize for saying mean things about you.*
>
> *A kid who just fell down and may have broken his leg.*
>
> *A cold winter day, standing at the bus stop with a little boy who doesn't have a coat.*

After each scenario, ask the following questions.

ASK:

• What would you do in this situation?

• How would your spiritual gifts help you do the right thing in this situation?

Once kids have acted out all the situations, continue.

ASK:

• Look at your spiritual gift cards. How can you use one of your gifts this week?

SAY:

The Holy Spirit has given each of you gifts that'll last a lifetime. Take your cards home and share your gifts with your family this week. Let's close in prayer.

PRAY:

Dear God, thank you for giving each of us gifts. We pray that you'll reveal to us, bit by bit, what our gifts are, so we can see how special you've made us. Thank you for taking the time to make every child in here unique and for helping us face challenges in life with these powerful gifts of the Spirit. In Jesus' name, amen.

Kids' Travel Guide™ Series

Kids' Travel Guide to the Parables

The parables of Jesus are rich resources for transforming children! This edition of the Kids' Travel Guide series explores 13 of Jesus' "greatest hits" parables. Lead kids (age levels K-5th grade) on a 13-week exploration of the parables that will help them understand what God wants of them. *Kids' Travel Guide to the Parables* includes "Pathway Points" to focus kids in on the point to each parable in fun and interactive ways. It's perfect for Sunday school or midweek, and **flexible**—works for 2 kids…12 kids…20 kids!

▶ ISBN 978-0-7644-7013-4 • $19.99 *In Canada $21.99*

Kids' Travel Guide to the Armor of God
▶ ISBN 978-0-7644-2695-7
$19.99 *In Canada $21.99*

Kids' Travel Guide to the 23rd Psalm
▶ ISBN 978-0-7644-4005-2
$19.99 *In Canada $21.99*

Kids' Travel Guide to the Fruit of the Spirit
▶ ISBN 978-0-7644-2390-1
$19.99 *In Canada $21.99*

Kids' Travel Guide to the Lord's Prayer
▶ ISBN 978-0-7644-2524-0
$19.99 *In Canada $21.99*

Kids' Travel Guide to the Ten Commandments
▶ ISBN 978-0-7644-2224
$19.99 *In Canada $21.99*

Each book includes 13 lessons with these fun features to help take your kids on a travel adventure:

- **In-Focus Verse** around which the adventure is focused.
- **Departure Prayer** designed for children to add their own words of prayer.
- **First-Stop Discoveries:** Narrated enactment or group activity exploring the lesson's Bible story.
- **Story Excursions:** Through Bible stories, bring the book's biblical theme to life in fun, imaginative, and dramatic ways.
- **Adventures in Growing:** Activities show kids how to apply what they've learned to their daily lives!
- **Souvenirs:** Kids create pages that go into a notebook (their very own travel journal!) to remind them of the lesson's Bible point.

Order today! Call 800.447.1070 or visit Group.com